Happy Birthday to . . . Who?

Happy Birthday to . . . Who?

The Definitive No Holds Barred Father's Guide to Surviving Kids' Birthday Parties

Howard Camner

Illustrated by: Cathy (Camner) Lowen

To order additional copies of this book, contact:
Xlibris
1-888-795-4274
www.Xlibris.com
Orders@Xlibris.com
794074

CONTENTS

Dedication vii

Introduction ix

You Have No Choice 1

The Invitation 5

The Gift 9

Going to a Birthday Party at Someone's House
Versus a Public Place 11

Finding the House 15

Attire 21

PARTY TIME 25

Dealing with Clowns and Other Characters 39

Pony Rides 47

Bounce House Blues 51

The Pinata 57

You Can Have Your Cake 63

Happy Birthday to...Who? 67

Exit Stage Left! 73

About the Author 83

About the Illustrator 83

DEDICATION

For my children, Judi and Eli, when they were children, and didn't understand the Hell I was going through taking them to birthday parties. To my darling wife, Sue, who forced me to surrender my freedom and sanity taking the aforementioned kids to birthday parties against my will, and especially to fathers of young children everywhere. May this book be your guiding light in a world gone mad.

INTRODUCTION

On November 9th of the year 2000, when my wife Sue handed me a piece of paper announcing that she was pregnant (I don't think we were speaking at the time) I was overjoyed. Anything I ever accomplished prior to that moment suddenly meant absolutely nothing, or at the most, very little. This child would be my masterpiece; my legacy. I was going to be a father. Someone would soon be calling me "Daddy".

Time staggered on, as it tends to do, and on July 5th of 2001, 18 minutes after the witching hour, Judi Rose came into the world. In the delivery room I was propped up in a chair so I wouldn't lose consciousness while standing, and a nurse put my newborn little girl in my lap. I looked at her with a love I could never have imagined, and she stuck her tongue out at me. That was the beginning. A year and a half later my son Elijah took his place as the rightful prince of the world, and I had my family.

Everything was wonderful and terrific, or so I thought. Then just before her second birthday, Judi was invited to her first birthday party. We went. It was cute. We left. Then she was invited to her second birthday party. We went. It was sort-of cute. We left. Then she was invited to her third birthday party where I started to realize that the same people were at the third birthday party that were at the first two birthday parties. Suddenly it wasn't so cute anymore. In fact, I was starting to get annoyed. Then *Eli* started getting invited to birthday parties. Now I was really getting annoyed. Soon my weekends were spent doing nothing but going to kids' birthday parties.

Every single weekend I am with the same people at different birthday parties. Often times there are two or more birthday parties a day and the same people move from one birthday party to the next birthday party. This is insanity at its highest level. Sometimes if someone screws up and birthday party times conflict, my wife takes one of the kids to one birthday party and I take the other kid to the other birthday party. I can't imagine the Hell that would have occurred if we had had three kids.

There was a time when I had goals and dreams for my life, but now all I do is go to birthday parties. When I'm at these birthday parties I've noticed that the kids have fun, the women yak it up, but the men are as lost as lost could be. They are absolutely miserable. They remind me of the last scenes of the 1962 cult classic "Carnival of Souls" where all the lifeless spirits just meander around aimlessly; their vital spark gone, their once twinkling eyes glazed over.

During the week, these guys are attorneys, doctors, high-powered businessmen, pillars of the community, big shots of all kinds, but on the weekends at these kids' birthday parties they are all lost tormented souls. They are all mere pitiful shadows of their former selves. It soon became obvious to me that these fathers need guidance. I scoured bookstores for something that would help, but there was nothing. Therefore this book was born out of necessity. It is at once a survival guide, an instruction manual, and a rant and a half. The poet John Donne wrote that no man is an island. This book is my attempt to reach out to my fellow fathers. It is my hope that it will bring us all together and will help to end our suffering. No one else has stepped forward. Therefore I feel it's my duty; no, my mission, to lead all fathers out of the darkness, the nightmare, that is children's birthday parties. This book will help us all survive.

YOU HAVE NO CHOICE

When you consummated your marriage and at some point while in ecstasy conceived your child, you automatically sentenced yourself to spend the next decade (at least) going to kids' birthday parties. Not just a few birthday parties, *hundreds* of birthday parties. That's right, hundreds. In short, you can kiss your weekends goodbye.

Your wife, that woman you entered into holy wedlock with, will take care of all the details. You don't even have to R.S.V.P. Your beloved bride will take care of that. All you have to do is show up. But showing up isn't just "showing up". Don't think you're getting off easy. There's a lot involved.

First of all, you *have* to show up. There's no alternative. There's no way out. You're cooked. If you don't show up your wife will hate you and will make the remainder of your time on this planet a journey through Hell that you can't imagine. Your child will *really* hate you and will announce it constantly, as in, "I hate you Daddy!!! I hate you!!!" You don't need that misery. Take the miserable path of least resistance. Go to the damned party.

THE INVITATION

(or, how do you even know there's a party?)

Your child will receive an invitation to the birthday party either in the mail or someone will hand it to your child or your wife directly. They will *not* give it to you under any circumstances. Why? Because they don't trust you pal. *You* will "accidentally" lose it or inadvertently toss it. It'll be one of those scenarios where you actually say "Oops!" aloud just before you actually do the deed, you cunning sob, you. The handoff might be at your child's school, after-school care, a social function, the supermarket, or even at another birthday party. It doesn't matter how the invitation gets to your kid or your wife. The upshot is, you're going.

The invitation itself usually has a theme to it which will be the theme of the birthday party. The theme usually comes directly from the birthday boy or girl's interest, be it pirates, princesses, dinosaurs (including Barney), Sesame Street, Power Rangers, and more princesses. The name of the child on the invitation will be prefaced with a title relating to the theme of the party: "Princess" Amy, "Pirate" Sammy, "Power Ranger" Alberto, etc. Don't try to figure out who the kid is. Your kid knows and your wife knows. You don't have a clue, and more to the point, you couldn't care less.

A side note: we know a family where the father runs a baseball camp for kids. That's what he does for a living. So whenever his kid has a birthday party, the theme is *always* baseball. The "party" is *always* a baseball game. I feel sorry for the kid. As anyone familiar with basic psychology knows, having the same birthday party theme year after year will eventually drive the kid over the edge and he'll rebel. Maybe the kid will become a football player or a drag queen or both. Never force a theme on a kid. The theme should be what the kid wants, not the parents.

THE GIFT

(you didn't think you were getting in free, did ya?)

Don't spend over five or ten bucks. The birthday boy or girl will receive lots of gifts and this isn't the place to outdo anyone. Whatever you give them is going to be broken two minutes after they unwrap it anyway, so don't waste your money. If you really want to get off cheap, you can not give them anything and claim that you did and claim that they lost it. But if you do want to get something and you're not sure what to get the kid, go with the theme of the invitation / birthday party. If the theme is "dinosaurs" for "T-Rex" Timmy, then that's what Timmy likes, so get Timmy a dinosaur toy. If the theme is "princesses" for "Princess" Patty's party (say that three times fast) then you get Patty a princess thing. You're not splitting the atom; just get the kid something cheap.

GOING TO A BIRTHDAY PARTY AT SOMEONE'S HOUSE VERSUS A PUBLIC PLACE

Fathers generally don't like going to kids' birthday parties for countless reasons. Maybe it's a "man thing", but men typically regard it as a total waste of valuable time. Time which could be better spent doing just about anything else; be it watching TV, staring at one's hand, poking through the fridge, or pondering how they get those little plastic things on the ends of shoelaces. Sure it's selfish and less than thoughtful, but that's just the way it is.

One of the biggest concerns about going to a kid's birthday party is the physical location where the party will be held. Will it be at a public place or at someone's house? That is always my first question when my wife informs me that I'll be going to another one. Personally, I dread going to people's houses which I'll explain shortly. Typical public places where kids' birthday parties are held include a "Party Place" where party rooms are rented out specifically to have parties, a park, or a kids' gym. I'm sure there are a few other places like bowling alleys and miniature golf courses, but from my vast experience in the field, these are the three biggies. Attending a party at a public place is the lesser of the two evils because it's a lot easier to sneak out of a public place than it is to sneak out of someone's house. If the party is at someone's house that's a world of trouble, because once you walk through that door, you are essentially, a prisoner.

ᏩINDING ᏆHE HOUSE

Your wife will hand (or toss) you the invitation with the address of the house on it. You're now expected to go to some stranger's house, enter it, and hang around while your kid has a wonderful time. But first you have to find the place. Once you get to the general vicinity (can't help you there) start looking for balloons tied to a pole or a mailbox. Then start looking for some frantic fellow father running around doing what his wife has instructed him to do. He is at his wits' end. Whatever you do, don't offer to help. It's a sure thing he'll take you up on it, if for no other reason, to have someone to talk to. Never forget, misery loves company.

But before you need to worry about that, you need to park the car. You'll see a bunch of cars parked at all angles. You'll be able to tell a lot from the cars alone. If there's a large crowd you may have to park some distance away. But no matter where you park, and I want you to pay very close attention here, ***make certain you cannot be blocked in***! If you get blocked in you're completely screwed. And if you had any escape plans, you can forget about it.

Another thing that could happen is that the house may be inside of a gated community where you have to go through a guard in order to get in. If you're like me you're hoping that the guard will forbid you from entering and you can call it a day. When you get to the guard, do your best to look your worst. Try to look like a hardcore criminal and hope he or she cares enough about their job to turn you away. That way you can at least tell your wife that you *tried* to get to the party.

ATTIRE

Chances are your wife will see how you're dressed before you leave your place, especially since she's going to toss (or hand) you the invitation with the address on it. If there's one thing I learned before I got booted out of the Boy Scouts it's this: be prepared. In your car you should have stashed a change of clothes that you will put on before arriving at the party. These clothes will make you look like you've been on a bus for three days after a prison break when you knocked out a derelict and traded your prison garb for his alley attire which he found in a dumpster behind a bad Chinese restaurant. You may even want to splash on a bit of Night Train as cologne to make yourself even more appealing. As an added feature, if you can get away with it at home, don't shower or shave for several days leading up to the birthday party. And whatever you do, do *not* put on any deodorant or brush your teeth before the party. That defeats the whole purpose. What

is the whole purpose? The idea here being that
when you say you have to leave, no one's going
to beg you to stay. Sure, they'll talk about you
when you're gone, but bad press is better than
no press.

PARSY SIME

(mingling, munching & looking for a way out)

If your child's in pre-school, regular school, or some kind of group, chances are you'll see the very same people at every single birthday party every single weekend, as I do. If I gave you a million dollars you wouldn't be able to tell me one of their names. Your wife knows their names. Your kid even knows some of their names. But you, you don't have a clue – and, once again, more to the point, you couldn't care less. For some reason, many of them know your name, but you don't know theirs. This can be uncomfortable, so here's what you do. If someone acknowledges your existence in any way, quickly greet them with a hearty handshake and an exuberant, "HOW THE HELL ARE YA?!" If there are kids within earshot you might want to omit the "Hell". Aw what the hell, leave it in. This quickly eliminates any guessing games as to who's who. It shows that you at least recall the face from the previous weekend.

As far as chit-chat goes, it can get as bad as bad can be at these birthday parties. Here now is a fine example of typical chit-chat between fathers who all long to be elsewhere. Our dialogue begins after a long period of awkward silence with the occasional yelling at a kid to stop doing this or that.

Father #1: Boy that sun sure is sunny!
Father #2: That's some sun.
Father #3: Remember that song "Let the Sun Shine In"? All the fathers nod, smiling, ready to blow their brains out.
Father #1: That was some song.
Father #2: Whatever happened to that song?

As far as chit-chat goes, I'm like Mr. Ed the talking horse. If I don't have something to say I don't say it. I could go the Groucho Marx route, but the goal is to get out of there, not to start a scene. Always remember that none of the fathers want to be there, so have sympathy. They're on your side and you're on theirs. You're part of a brotherhood of trapped men who want nothing more than to be somewhere else. So if a fellow father tries to make small talk, be kind and talk. If you really don't want to be bothered and prefer to daydream about being on a beach with a couple of blondes feeding you grapes, just talk about something mundane like the weather or your prostate problems. Just bore him to death and he'll leave. If he wants to hear more about your prostate problems, just grab your kid and go.

By the way, at these parties if you're acknowledged at all, it will be in the third person by both the adults and the children. You will be addressed and referred to as "<u>YOUR CHILD'S NAME HERE</u>'s daddy". For example, my kids are Judi and Eli. A parent won't talk to me directly. Why? Well I'm told I "scare people". Whatever the hell that means. I'm not bad-looking, it's my "I don't want to be here" demeanor that puts people off. I use it everywhere I go. Anyway I could be three feet away and a parent will tell their child, "Go ask <u>Judi's daddy</u> where Judi's mommy is." Whereas a kid will get right in my face all grimy and excited and pant, "Eli's daddy! Eli's daddy! I ate a frog!"

At least the frog got away from the party.

Speaking of eating, the food at kids' birthday parties is usually crap. Typically it's bad plain cheese pizza, tortilla chips and watered-down apple juice. Sometimes there's ham croquettes and bizarre finger sandwiches with some kind of florescent neon pinkish spread inside that looks like a science experiment gone terribly awry. Often times there are flies circling the food to add to the appeal. I'm waiting for the moment when one of those flies sucks up some of that florescent neon pinkish spread. There's going to be a monster the likes of which cannot be imagined.

If you absolutely have to eat, make damned sure you're first in line. If you're not first in line, don't even think about putting any of that garbage in your mouth. Between the flies doing whatever they do to it, and the other party-goers touching every single thing on the platter before they select the one that feels right to the touch, you'll be putting every germ known to science, and then some, into your body. Don't risk your life. Your body is your temple, or whatever they say.

Speaking of bodies, you may see a few of those that grab your attention. Maybe the lone mother of another kid, the birthday kid's attractive aunt, an older female cousin, a sexy neighbor, and so forth. There's usually a few of those who show up. Forget about it! Stay focused! You're not there to look at broads. You're there to leave. Remember, you may not know who these people are, but they know who you are, and that kind of problem you don't need.

Let's get back to the party food. Here now is a partial list of diseases and illnesses you can easily acquire from eating kids' birthday party food. You can get a lot of infections from eating that fine cuisine. The infections usually involve becoming very intimate with the head, and I don't mean the one on your shoulders. And that would be getting off easy. There's always a hospital bed waiting. The bacterium to watch out for have those crazy scientific doctor-type names that no one can understand, such as "Campylobacter", "Salmonella" (we heard of that one), "E. coli 0157H7" (we heard of E. coli, but not the 0157H7 bit), "Calicivirus" also called "Norwalk-like virus". There are also infections caused by "Shigella", "Hepatitis A", "Giardia lamblia" and the ever-popular "Cryptosporidia".

I won't go into the disgusting nasty horrific problems that these things can cause. It's just too sickening to even write about. Plus, there are always toxins and other poisonous chemicals that can get into kids' birthday party food by accident. Even strep throat (a childhood favorite) can be passed via food. But let's not get crazy here. The point is, it can happen. So why run the risk just to be sociable? Just do yourself a favor and don't get near the garbage they serve at kids' birthday parties.

Refrain from eating until you leave the party. And if you're "starving", you're not starving. Those people you see on the cover of National Geographic who live in the desert where there's no water and nothing could possibly grow are starving. Don't eat anything. Just bite the bullet and wait it out. The only other option you have is to wait until everyone's out of the kitchen and poke through the fridge. It's a pretty gutsy move and it takes someone who flat out doesn't care about anything. If you get caught, which you probably will, you can always say that you were deeply concerned about the host family's health and were checking the food in the fridge for the previously mentioned bacterium. It would help to have the list with you so you can rattle off all the horrifying possibilities. That way you'll truly be appreciated for your concern and admired for your superior knowledge.

Now your kid's another story. You can't stop your kid from eating that crap, or again, you'll catch hell from all directions. So don't even try. Of course if you see an army of flies on something Junior's reaching for, you can strongly suggest an alternative snack.

A CAUTIONARY NOTE: Another problem with going to someone's house for the birthday party is that you may be tempted to steal something. Even though this kind of thought might not normally ever enter your mind, this is a different situation. You're angry about being there in the first place and you want to strike back at society. Sure, you could buy a high-powered automatic rifle on the black market and climb a water tower and go nuts, but that's too Hollywood, it's not the real you. And the headlines would make you look like a real schmuck: "MAN GOES BERSERK FROM ATTENDING TOO MANY BIRTHDAY PARTIES". This is not the way you want to be remembered. So you might consider resorting to a little larceny. But don't do it. It's simply not appropriate and it makes you a bad role model for your kid; "Daddy, where did you get the porcelain poodle?" Plus you know damned well that if they notice something missing and run down the list of possible suspects, they'll figure out it's you, the disgruntled guy, who did the dirty deed. Then word will quickly spread that you're a no-good thief and you'll never be invited to another birthday party ag- HEY! We may need to reconsider this.

So how did your nightmare really begin? It started in the early 1800s when pompous arrogant hypocritical anal-retentive Victorians with fat wallets used their kid's birthday parties to show the neighborhood how well-stuffed they were. But the main purpose of the parties was to teach the little bastards manners so they knew how to act when they took their place in "high society". In other words, the original purpose of kids' birthday parties was to teach these rich spoiled brats (notice I didn't call them "bastards" again) how to be very polite pompous pricks when they got older. But thankfully, things have changed, and people don't have to wear Victorian clothes anymore.

DEALING WITH CLOWNS AND OTHER CHARACTERS

A lot of these birthday parties have clowns or characters that make a special appearance to the delight of one and all – except maybe you. Pity the performer. Remember, "Elmo" doesn't want to be there either. In fact, "Elmo" doesn't want to be there a lot more than you don't want to be there, and as we both know, that's saying quite a lot. "Elmo" wants to go home or to the nearest watering hole a hundred times worse than you do. But the poor bastard needs money. He may have a nagging wife or a cocaine habit or maybe he's just some single cat trying to pay some bills. Do you think it's fun suffocating in that ridiculous costume in 120 degree heat? Not to mention putting on some kind of "show" and having a bunch of snotty brats clawing at you. It's a rough gig. Plus, they face the possibility that the offspring of some prick lawyer is going to notice and announce to everyone that "Elmo" doesn't exactly "look right". There's a reason for that. It's called "trademark infringement".

If you're a lawyer you can skip this part because I may not have my facts straight, but if you're not a lawyer, read on. Infringement occurs when one party, such as the company our birthday party "Elmo" works for, uses a trademarked property which is "confusingly similar" or completely identical to a trademarked property such as the "real Elmo" which is owned by another company. Let's say, oh I don't know, Sesame Street for example. In other words if birthday party "Elmo" looks exactly like the "real Elmo" and Sesame Street finds out about it, they could get grouchy and take birthday party Elmo's company's ass to court. And there could be some asshole like me snapping photos of birthday party "Elmo" and sending those photos to the producers of Sesame Street along with pertinent information hoping there will be a major lawsuit and word will spread about what a rotten person I am for taking and sending those photos. And who knows? I might be banned from any and all kids' birthday parties for eternity. This by coincidence happens to be my objective.

To avoid infringement suits, the character companies use cheap mock-up costumes that look like they've been in every Thanksgiving Day parade since the first Thanksgiving when the Pilgrims sat down with the Indians at Macys and have never once been cleaned. They throw a red rug over some poor putz, sew two Ping-Pong balls on it for eyes, (Ping-Pong is trademarked by the way, which you didn't know) and call it "Elmo". They think kids won't know the difference. Bullshit! Kids know everything, and they know that a red rug with two Ping-Pong balls attached, does not an Elmo make.

More words of wisdom: If it looks at any time like the clown, magician, or character is going to bring you up to participate in the act and you're just not interested in having those snotty little rodents laughing at you to add insult to injury, just start picking your nose or scratching your sack (or both simultaneously, which isn't easy, I'm told) and he'll go to someone else to be the buffoon. If he doesn't go to someone else, that means there's a real prick inside that costume and you could and should "accidentally" cause him some real pain. How you do that is up to you. You have my permission to do it, just be careful and creative. That's all I ask.

PONYRIDES

(watch your step)

Some birthday parties you attend will have pony rides. This is considered extravagant in a cheesy sort of way. Pony rides work on two different levels for you. Let's start with the second level first. You can take this opportunity to stop feeling sorry for yourself because your day is shot to hell, and you can and should feel sorry for the ponies. Pity the ponies! These poor innocent creatures are essentially made into tortured and sometimes beaten slaves for entertainment purposes. They have to carry these brats around on their backs in the blistering heat and there's always some grossly overweight punk who thinks he's the Lone Ranger and sidekicks the crap out of these poor animals. Personally I like to see kids like this thrown off and trampled by the sweet ponies. But that's just me.

That was the second thing, here's number one. The pony rides may be your lawsuit. I'm not saying to go to a kid's birthday party looking to sue, but don't totally reject the idea simply because they were kind enough to invite you. They *didn't* invite you. They invited your kid. We'll get more into the idea of suing your host later. The pony ride is a good suit because God-forbid something happens to your precious child, you can bypass your host and sue the pony guy directly. You can sue for a number of mishaps. You know the obvious ones. Here's one that might not occur to you. It's a biological fact that ponies crap everywhere. Maybe you or yours could "accidentally" step in some pony poo, slip, slide, and break a leg or two. (Now that's poetry!)

I don't want to sound cruel; I'm just trying to help. What you could do instead of breaking a leg is to *pretend* to break a leg and scream. Then you find a good doctor and slip him some cash to put a cast on you. These guys are in it for the money anyway aren't they? They didn't become doctors because of their love, compassion and concern for their fellow human beings. If that's what you think, compare your car to theirs. Remember the pony guy doesn't speak a word of English, so he won't know what's going on until you scream bloody murder. Music isn't the international language; screaming in agony is. Anyone can understand it, even the pony guy.

Once you scream, the pony guy will know there's a problem. A problem his pony caused. Some countries in the world have strange customs. For all you know that pony your kid has been riding on is the guy's wife. You just don't know. There's one more thing to consider if you do plan to sue the pony guy. Those ponies may be all he has in the world. So if you sue him and you win the suit, guess who's gonna be giving pony rides?

BOUNCE HOUSE BLUES

(really lookin' for that lawsuit)

There's a zillion things that can go wrong at a kid's birthday party. So if you could use a few hundred grand keep your eyes peeled. Of course you don't want anything to happen to your precious offspring, but if it'll get you that totally restored mint condition 1960 Corvette convertible like the one in the old "Route 66" TV series that you saw an ad for on the internet, then what the hell?

You've suffered for your kid long enough, he can suffer for you. The best place for a "problem" to happen is in the "Bounce House". If you don't know, a "Bounce House" is a huge inflatable balloon-like "house" with a rugged balloon like "floor" similar in theory to a trampoline, that kids bounce on. And kids *love* to bounce.

It used to be an extravagant item to have at a birthday party, but is now "typical", swiftly approaching "humdrum", and "boring" is looming large on the horizon. An external blower motor keeps the air flowing into the Bounce House. Certainly the external motor is a danger, plus the attached extension cord to the house is another danger. Not to mention the inherent danger of a bunch of kids bouncing together. That's three very dangerous dangers! I've never seen anyone sign a waiver walking into a birthday party, so keep one eye on your kid and the other on that Vette.

Sometimes the Bounce House will collapse for whatever reason. I've been a witness to this on several occasions. When the Bounce House collapses, this would be a superb opportunity to have your kid scream like he or she has never screamed before. In fact, it might be a good idea to rehearse the screams when Mom is nowhere around. But be careful that your kid doesn't go hoarse from the rehearsals. That would mess up everything. So when the Bounce House collapses, have your kid scream like they're being attacked by this giant rubber monstrosity. Think bad B movie monsters. Then you want to keep reminding your kid of the horror of it all daily, so the memory of it will impede their ability to succeed in life. You should be able to collect some real coin on that one. But remember, and this is important, your kid has to be *inside* the Bounce House in order for your claim to hold water.

A side note about the Bounce House. You'll appreciate the Bounce House not only for its potential for disaster and your subsequent lawsuit, but also because every once in a while one of those lone mothers of another kid, or the birthday kid's attractive aunt, or older female cousin, or that sexy neighbor who's got the goods, might decide to lose their inhibitions, summon their inner child, and bounce in the Bounce House. Watch yourself Romeo. Watch what you're watching. Remember, you don't know who these people are, but they know who you are. I can't stress that enough.

If you get caught watching some woman bounce with just a little too much interest (which of course will be by someone who's friendly with your wife who has been watching *you* and expecting this) just pretend you're admiring the strength of the material that the Bounce House is constructed of. I suggest making a comment loud enough to be heard by several people, such as, "Look how strong this material is that this Bounce House is constructed of." Your wife's friend won't buy it, but at least you can claim that you said it, and you'll have witnesses.

THE PIÑATA

(or, let's teach them how to break things)

Most people think the piñata is a Mexican contribution, but it really came from China where it was used to celebrate the arrival of spring in that town. Marco Polo (the guy, not the game) discovered it in China and showed it to the Spanish, the Italians, and the French, who although they liked the idea of hanging something and then beating it, could take it or leave it. But the Spaniards were thrilled by it and brought it over to Mexico because they weren't *that* thrilled by it. The Mexicans loved it because they like that sort of thing. And since Mexico is closer to us than China, we think it's Mexican.

Originally, piñatas had points that stuck out. Each point on the piñata represented a sin. The stick used to break the piñata represented love. And since love conquers all, the stick destroyed the sins. The person with the stick was supposed to resolve to be a better person before he hit the piñata. You follow? When the first piñatas (circa 14th century) were busted open, seeds spilled out. When people saw that those 14th century brats weren't exactly in ecstasy with the seeds, they changed the contents of the piñatas to sweets and fruit. Today there are no sins associated with the piñata, but there definitely should be. There's a whole long history to the piñata which I don't have the time or the patience for. If you're that enthralled, feel free to look it up yourself with my blessings. And you also might want to consider a hobby or a rest home.

These days, piñatas are shaped like cartoon characters, clown figures, footballs, bugs, and whatever else they can dream up. Those hosts that take the piñata a little too seriously and a little too far, blindfold the kid with the love-stick and tell him to swing it as hard as he can to break open the piñata. That's real smart. Have a blindfolded kid swinging a stick with a bunch of other little kids gathered around. On the other hand, this little tradition could be that gold mine of a lawsuit we've been hoping for. If you or your precious offspring gets clobbered by Junior wielding his love-stick, I'd say it's lawyer time. In fact, I would call it "attempted murder".

The smart party hosts don't use the "blindfolded punk with a stick" method to bust open the piñata. The smart ones have the piñatas where all the kids get a long streaming ribbon to pull on. At the count of three they all pull at the same time and absolutely nothing happens. They repeat it and repeat it until finally the father of the birthday kid (who at this point wants everyone out of his yard) puts down his video camera, to his wife's dismay, and rips the piñata apart with his bare hands so all the stuff falls out of it. To the kids and their fathers, he's a hero. To his wife and the other women, he's the devil in Bermuda shorts because he just loused up a tradition.

Now all the kids have been given little plastic bags in which to collect the loot that falls out of the piñata. When it does fall out, there is a mad free-for-all as they scoop up the loot and put it in their bags. The "loot" is crap with a capital "C". Thus, it would be spelled "Crap". There's old candy that's been sitting inside that piñata for God knows how long, and some very cheap trinkets such as: ultra-cheap plastic rings that don't fit, little bouncing balls that don't bounce, cheap temporary tattoos that don't stick, crummy plastic whistles that don't blow, cheap spinning tops that don't spin, lousy plastic mazes where the ball won't go into the hole, and cheap compasses that always point south. But fear not my friend, the end is near. You'll soon be pointing yourself and your kid toward the exit door, and that should work quite well.

YOU CAN HAVE YOUR CAKE

(but don't eat it)

When you hear someone announce that it's time for the birthday cake, you can start breathing easy. The reason you can start breathing easy is because you can bolt right after your kid is finished with his piece. Don't try to stop your kid from eating the cake. They live for that. If *you* want to continue living, when the host or one of the mothers shoves a piece of cake in your face, refuse it. Make up something quick, such as, "I'm full, thanks." If they comment that they've noticed you haven't eaten a thing since you've been there, (and this may come from your wife's friend who was watching you watch the other broads bounce in the Bounce House) just say that you ate before you got there. If they then ask what you ate before you got there, they have officially crossed the line, and you can then legally and morally tell them to go screw themselves.

If you find yourself waiting forever to hear someone announce that it's time for the cake and no one's making the announcement, then just go ahead and do it yourself. There are two ways to go about this. If you're feeling exceptionally pissed off about having to blow your day and you're not crazy about your surroundings or anyone in your surroundings, just come out and announce, **"CAKE!"**

By using the one word "cake", you're not breaking any sacred rules. You didn't say, "Ladies and Gentlemen, boys and girls, it is now time for the birthday cake." All you said was "cake". That doesn't mean anything by itself. It's a lone noun. There's no verb nearby to give it meaning. But it's the word that the other fathers and all the kids have been praying for (for different reasons). And you just became their hero.

The other way is to start a rumor. Don't start with a woman because it'll stop with her. Why? Because every woman there knows better and they don't trust you anyway. Start with a fellow father. Preferably one who has been bitching and moaning that he's missing a football game. Just lean over to him and softly say, "I heard they're ready to serve the cake." Then just sit back and relax. He'll handle the rest. Personally I've announced that it was time for the cake the moment I got to the party. If I'm with my wife, she'll just roll her eyes and comment publicly that I'm an idiot. If it's just me with my offspring, *others* will roll their eyes and comment that I'm an idiot. And my plan to leave quickly is foiled and I have to resort to other methods as laid out in this book. We do what we must to survive. Speaking of surviving, for a quick review of why you shouldn't eat the cake, see the "diseases and illnesses you can catch from kids' birthday party food" list again.

HAPPY BIRTHDAY TO...WHO?

Once everyone's gathered around the cake shooing flies, and the birthday kid is perched in front of it, and the candles are finally lit after an 18 minute quest for matches and 12 minutes of trying to light the damned things, it is now time to sing the birthday song. I don't mean you. You're not going to actually sing. You're going to mouth the words.

If you don't know, and I'm sure you don't, because I didn't and if I didn't, there's no way that you did, the classic "Happy Birthday to You" song was composed by two sisters from Kentucky, Patty and Mildred Hill. Patty Hill (sounds like a place where cows graze, doesn't it?) was born in 1868 and was a schoolteacher. She wrote the original words. Mildred, born in 1859, was also a teacher and a composer. Mildred came up with the melody. Sounds like these broads needed a little sausage on their pizza. The lyric Patty wrote was originally for a classroom greeting song called "Good Morning to All" that those wild Hill sisters published in a book called <u>Song Stories for the Kindergarten</u> in 1893. The lyric later changed to "Good Morning to You" and then changed again to "Happy Birthday to You". Hopefully they'll change again because I am so sick of hearing that damned song I can't tell you. The misery that those two women have put me through defies description. The Happy Birthday Song didn't really become a fixture at birthday parties until it was featured in Irving Berlin's 1934 Broadway musical "As Thousands Cheer", then people started singing it all the time at birthday parties. But why use that annoying song? There are many other Broadway tunes that could have been used. Why not, "I Go to Rio", "Old Devil Moon" or "Oklahoma"? Thank you, Irving. Thanks a lot.

As far as "singing" the birthday song, remember, you won't know the birthday kid's name, and more importantly, you don't give a crap, so be careful! I suggest standing away from everyone else, but if you're caught in the crowd and it looks like you have to "sing along", just mumble the word "Ambah" when it's time to sing the kid's name. Through a lot of trial and error I've discovered that the word "Ambah" when mumbled sounds like any kid's name.

Another thing that might help is this: there's usually at least one frustrated opera singer who thinks he's Luciano Pavarotti. It's either a grandfather who spent a little time in a strait jacket years back, or a deranged uncle recently released from prison where he did a lot of singing in the shower. These guys are a blessing because everyone will turn and look at them and you won't even have to pretend to sing.

But just in case Mr. Pavarotti doesn't make the scene, here now are the words to the Happy Birthday Song you will pretend to sing. Please note: this isn't The Beatles' version from the White Album, this is the traditional version by the Hill sisters, so don't get excited. Well, truth be told, we're not sure who wrote the actual Happy Birthday Song. We do believe it was the Hill sisters, Patty and Mildred. And we do know that another Hill sister, Jessica Hill, sued somebody for stealing Mildred's melody. It's a great mystery that I don't give a rat's ass about, and either do you, so here we go:

Happy birthday to you
Happy birthday to you
Happy birthday dear...<u>Ambahhhh</u>
Happy birthday to you!

Wow! Someone obviously burnt the midnight oil creating that brilliant piece of literature!

EXIT STAGE LEFT!

(or right, as long as it sets you free, who cares where the exit is)

If you just can't stand it anymore and you need to bow out early, you'll have to either slip out the door with your kid unnoticed (good luck), or you'll need to approach your host with an excuse as to why you have to leave early. Here now are 25 sure-fire excuses to leave a kid's birthday party early. You may use them freely, but if you want to send me a few bucks to show your appreciation that's okay too. None of them have ever worked for me (except for #25). Maybe they'll work for you.

1. <u>YOUR CHILD'S NAME HERE</u> doesn't feel as well as he/she's acting. We have to go now.
2. I forgot I have a bill due, and if I don't pay it today, I'll be hit with a late fee.

3.   I'm sorry, but with all the problems in the world, I just can't feel joy right now.

4.   We have to go before I get a flat tire.

5.   I'm psychic and I just had a premonition that something's about to go wrong at home. We have to go, and fast!

6.   I heard an asteroid is barreling toward Earth and I have to put up the shutters.

7.   I think I saw a "wanted" poster of the clown at the post office. It's not safe here.

8.   I forgot to feed my Venus's-flytrap. If I don't leave now it'll die.

9.   (And along the same lines) I pulled enough flies off the cake to feed my Venus's-flytrap for 10 years. Thanks for inviting us.

10. These photographs on the wall of your family are scaring my kid. We have to go now.

11. I broke a mirror yesterday and I think I'm bad luck to be around. If I was selfish I would stay but....

12. (approach your host wiping your eyes) This birthday party is bringing back memories of my own childhood, when I was truly happy. It's just too emotional for me here.

13. My moon is in the Seventh House, and that's not easy to handle at a birthday party. Maybe next year I can do this, but not now.

14. (pull the host aside for this one) I see someone I saw do something he shouldn't have done and I don't want him to see me because he saw me see him, so I have to go.

15. I'm under house arrest and I'm breaking the law by being here. So to prove that I'm a good citizen I have to go now.

16. I'm having an argument with my wife tonight and I have to learn my lines.

17. Wouldn't you know it? The only place I could find to park was a "No Parking Zone". We really can't stay.

18. I just got a call that my kid might be very contagious, and with medical science still stumped for a cure, we should probably go.

19. My son keeps calling the Bounce House "a giant condom". I think this party is a bad influence on him.

20. I think the balloons are made of latex and I'm allergic to latex (if you know what I mean).

21. Most of the women and some of the men here are making a play for me, and I'm a married man, so I should go.

22. I draw the line at chocolate-covered pizza. We're leaving.

23. I heard "musical chairs" is next. I've seen kids get crushed, maimed, and mutilated playing that game. I'm sorry, but we won't stay for that.

24. If this is the best you can do, you can't expect us to celebrate a day that will haunt your child forever. Goodbye.

25. If you're really desperate to scram, put the burden of getting rid of you on your host. Do what I do. This won't work in a public setting, but if the birthday party's at someone's house, here's your ticket out. Walk up to the host and matter-of-factly ask where they keep the jewelry. You'll be out of there in no time. It works like a charm.

When you're actually ready to leave, don't even think about saying goodbye to more than one person. You could be there another two hours just saying goodbye. You could get sucked into mindless conversations with people who know they're trapped and envy you for attempting to escape. Remember, misery loves company. It's best to single out the host and say your adieu. Make sure you have your kid say "thank you" because your wife will certainly ask if that little exchange took place. And if it didn't, you're in for some hell partner.

If you **REALLY** want to cross the Styx into Hades, I mean a stay in Purgatory with no end in sight, leave the party without your kid getting a "goody bag". If you remember one thing from this book, let it be this:

DO NOT FORGET THE GOODY BAG!

You do that, and you'll be Public Enemy Number One to both child and spouse for the rest of your days on this planet. The goody bag is vital because it acts as hardcore proof that you actually went to the birthday party. Of course you could ask a fellow father who you know is going, to swipe you one and meet you at the corner for the handoff, but even *I'm* not that scummy. So don't forget the goody bag, and I cannot stress this enough: *MAKE SURE YOUR WIFE SEES IT*!!!

You're asking yourself, what is a goody bag? Allow me to explain. A goody bag is a bag that kids get when they leave a birthday party. Inside the bag is more crap: a defective whistle, old candy, a bendable animal of some mysterious species, some kind of squishy thing that defies definition, a little plastic magnifying glass that doesn't magnify, a little Martian figure, a pencil, and of course the always popular bubble soap with the circular wand that you can't get out of the plastic bottle without spilling out the soap which you will slip on and break your ass. This stuff will all be lost or broken two seconds after your kid dumps the bag on the floor at home.

There are times when you might see something in your kid's goody bag that you might want to keep for yourself. Maybe something that reminds you of your own childhood, or something you can actually use, like the pencil. Just explain to your kid that it's dangerous and confiscate it for their own protection. But make sure the wife's not around when you do that. Use common sense.

And finally, if it's your own kid's birthday party, you'll be pulling "Daddy Duty". That often involves holding a video camera, smiling like you're happy, and doing everything your wife instructs you to do. And that's quite a lot. Good luck Brother. You'll need it.

ABOUT THE AUTHOR

Howard Camner is a disgruntled father who was constantly forced to go to birthday parties when his children were children. He is also the author of 18 poetry books, an autobiography, and the creator, producer, and host of the now defunct comedy cable TV show "Life is a 4 Letter Word". He tries to survive in Miami, Florida, with his wife and children. He also has a single-wide lake mansion in Interlachen, Florida, that he escapes to whenever possible.

ABOUT THE ILLUSTRATOR

Cathy (Camner) Lowen enjoyed a career in art and design for many years before retiring to travel with her husband. The only time she has come out of retirement is when her brother asked her to illustrate this book. Cathy was once cajoled into face painting at a children's birthday party because the actual face painter was smart enough not to show up. While at the party she noticed how miserable the fathers were. They refused to have their faces painted.

Cathy is based in Seattle, when she is not traveling the planet.

NOV 1962

The author and illustrator